THE POWER OF

The NEUROSCIENCE of POSITIVE AFFIRMATIONS

By Shawn, Shayne, and Genein Letford, M.Ed

Illustrated by Victoria Mappala

To my Tia Belen, who helped me know who I AM. –Shawn T. Letford

I dedicate this book to my father, Albert Joseph Jefferson III, who always knew the power of I AM and taught this practice to his students around the world. I miss you and will carry on your work. – Genein Marie Letford

To my family, Jay, Alex, and Lily. Thank you for being with me through it all, and inspiring me to create. – Victoria Mappala

...

Forward

What is your I AM?

The Power of I AM has been written for all those who think they know, and those who do not yet know the power of I AM. For those who want to gain or deepen their understanding, this book, written by Genein M. Letford and her family, will provide insights and answers into your I AM. Over years of intentional self-searching and research into the Identity of Self, and with the help of this book, I believe that I have become present to the truth of the power of I AM. Two words, that when spoken with Knowledge and Belief...CREATE.

The words spoken after I AM create your realities, whether true or false, whether believed or denied. Delve into this book with a sincere desire to better see, to hear, and to know thy self, and thus be seen, be heard, and be known.

What is your I AM?

Mine..."**I AM GENEROUS.**"

-Earl Ameen, CEO Business Coach, Owl Enterprises

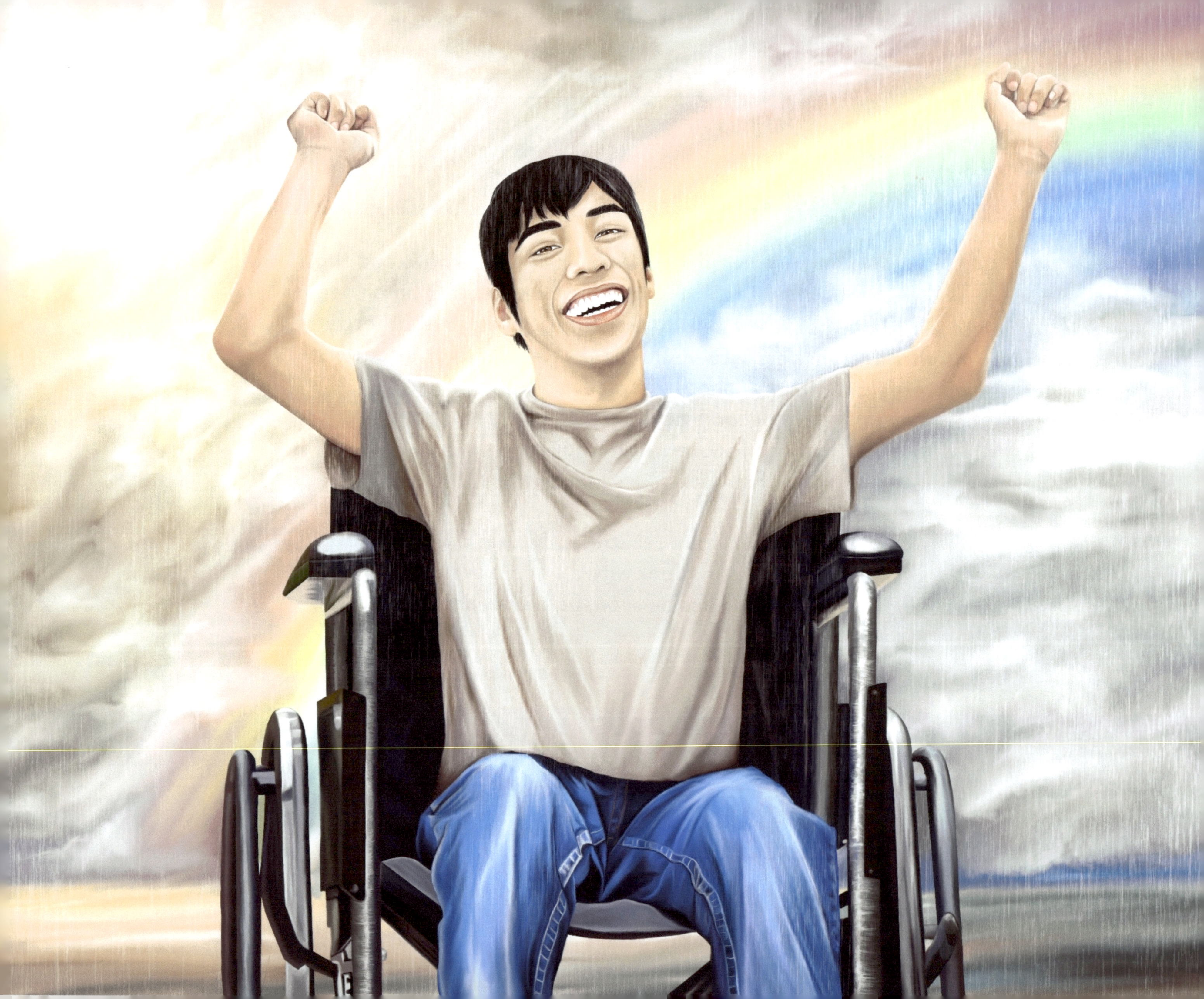

I am

Blessed

I am Worthy

I am

Loved

I am Healthy

12

I am
Wealthy

I am KIND

I am
Compassionate

I AM
BOLD

I am
Respectful

I AM
DILIGENT

Thank You
I AM CREATIVE
I am creative in every single way!

I am

Thankful

I am
Curious

I am
Confident

I AM
OBSERVANT

I am Adventurous

"And today I was,

and still AM
Creative!"

Dear Parents, Teachers, Leaders and Caregivers,

YOU ARE POWERFUL! And so are your words! My family is honored to share this work with you while introducing our illustrator, Mrs. Victoria Mappala, with her first illustrated book as an 'Inner Child' and children's book illustrator.

THE POWER OF I AM looks like a children's book, but we call our children's books 'Inner Child' books because our books are meant for adults as well as for children. Our 'Inner Child' books are for anyone who needs to discover, or rediscover, new elements of themselves and see the possibility of their creativity within their social and cultural environments. This is for adults who need to reconnect to their creative and confident inner power.

Our family, the founders of Intercultural Creativity® and NeuroSomatic Creativity®, believes that creativity and social, emotional, and academic intelligence can improve when we know, understand, and utilize our brains to the best of our ability.

With the advancement of fMRI technology and now, the more transportable fNIRS technology, we can better understand what our brains are doing inside our heads and while in concert with other brains. This is true with the thoughts we think and the words we speak to others and to ourselves. Let's jump in to learn why what we say to ourselves (and how we say it) has more of an effect on our identity, creativity, and success than we ever realized before.

BUILDING A POWERFUL BRAIN

Building. Such a powerful word. When we are building something, we have intention and, at most times, a blueprint. We hopefully have an idea of what success looks like. Just like building a house, when we build our identity (or rebuild for us older individuals), we build from the bottom up. Foundation is paramount. I honestly believe the words we are surrounded by early in childhood help build this foundation that we must stand upon while we live out this journey called life. The beauty of the word 'build' is that it is a verb. It is an action word. We get to be a part of this building for our children, our students, our team members, and ourselves.

"Words--so innocent and powerless as they are, as standing in a dictionary, how potent for good and evil they become in the hands of one who knows how to combine them."
-Nathaniel Hawthorn, American Novelist

LEVELS OF CONSCIOUSNESS

The brain is beautiful yet so mysterious. Driven by innovative technologies and new approaches in the field of neuroscience, our understanding of the brain--and what it means to be human--is coming into sharper focus. Learning how to better build your brain means understanding how your brain operates. The human brain is still one of the largest mysteries known to us. As mentioned above, technology is just now revealing some of the hidden treasures to neuroscientists since the turn of the century. In 2001, I remember climbing into my first fMRI machine for a research study led by my UCLA professor, Dr. Matthew Lieberman. Modern neuroscience was on the sunrise of a new era at that time, and I desired to be a part of the neural adventure in any form I could. I longed to understand the fueling force behind the connection of my brain, my mind, and my body. How did these connections make me ... me?

One of the first things I learned was that there are multiple levels of the mind. Per neuroscientist Dr. Caroline Leaf, the mind has three parts of consciousness, with the largest part being the nonconscious mind. The nonconscious mind is massive and never shuts down. It is very intelligent, fast, and can work on multiple things at once to keep us functioning and living life. It wants to keep us balanced, so it's always monitoring our existing thoughts and memories. It is aware of what could be worrisome to us.

When our massive nonconscious mind finds a worrying thought, it sends it up through the second part of the mind, the subconscious mind, which acts as a bridge between the nonconscious mind and the conscious mind. Several neuroscientists believe it is our mind below our consciousness, our subconscious and nonconscious mind, that actually drives our behavior.

It reminds me of the words of neuroscientist Dr. David Eagleman who said, "Your subconscious mind is running the show. Your conscious mind is like the broom closet in the mansion that is your brain!"

Dr. Leaf claims that our nonconscious and subconscious minds feed information into the conscious mind which shows up physically as what we feel, say, and do. It manifests itself in our behavior. This influences our perspectives and how we perceive the world.

Though our nonconscious mind is always on, our conscious mind isn't. It wakes up when we wake up! It is much slower as well. Our conscious mind is only able to focus on and process 5-10% of what we are exposed to, while the nonconscious can process up to 90-95%. Knowing this, successful adult leaders, as well as our young leaders, learn how to tap into their lower levels of the mind and get them in line for positive outcomes and strong mental, emotional and resilient health.

This is where mind management comes in. But before we can manage our mind, it is first important to know how our mind and brain are set up to operate. Understand that the biggest part of your mind, the part we are unaware of, is actually calling the plays and running the show! This is one of the first steps to beginning our mind management journey. Words (the words you say and are said around you) set the foundation for you to walk your first step in this journey of life.

THE POWER OF OUR WORDS

'Sticks and stones may break my bones, but words can never hurt me.'

Do you remember saying this? I do! This childhood ditty has attempted to lessen the hurtful residue of naysayers and bullies, but little did we know this phrase was so off the mark.

Words can hurt. Words do hurt.

You may not see the effects of it like seeing the physical effects of stones or a stick, but words can leave a mark on you internally. In fact, words can change your brain. Literally.

The spoken word is invisible. Likewise, many of the world's most powerful forces are also invisible, such as gravity, electricity, and magnetism to name a few. Dr. Nina Kraus, a sound neuroscientist from Northwestern University, claims that sound has a profound impact on our nervous system. Sound is a powerful and invisible force that is essential for human communication. We don't think that it is so important because we can't see them. We can't see the words. They are invisible as they enter into us, but their effect on us is undeniable.

In the book, *7½ Lessons About the Brains*, neuroscientist Dr. Lisa Feldman Barrett explains that we have a metabolic body budget. Just like a home financial plan has a financial budget to track income and outgoing expenses, our body has a budget, not of dollar bills but of metabolic energy. Our body budget directs resources and energy and is meant to keep all of your organs and systems functioning at their best. But did you know this? Our body budget can be manipulated by words; words you say to yourself and words others say to you.

Just think about it.

After having a tough loss at work or losing a sporting event, when a parent or coach comes up to encourage you, do you feel a change in your body? Do you feel recharged? That is your nervous system being affected by external words. If you have a big interview and before you walk into the interview room, you look in the bathroom mirror, stand up tall, and say, "I can do this! I AM capable!" Do you feel a change in your physicality? That's the power of words on your brain and your metabolic budget.

It can happen the other way as well. If someone you admire yells hurtful words to you, and you internalize them, it can affect your mind, your brain and your body budget.

Though invisible, words have a large effect on where energy flows and on how we view ourselves, how we view others, and how we view social situations.

We then can ask the question, "Why do the words we use, and the words others use with us, have such an impact on the inside of us?" Well, Dr. Barrett explains, "Because many brain regions that process language also control the insides of your body, including major organs and systems that support your body budget. These brain regions, which are contained in what scientists call the 'language network', guide your heart rate up and down. They adjust the glucose (sugars) entering your bloodstream to fuel your cells. They change the flow of chemicals that support your immune system. The power of words is not a metaphor. It's in your brain wiring."

Though our words are invisible, they are extremely powerful and have a huge effect on how we regulate our systems and shape our identities. We can now intentionally use the power of words to build our brains, and the brains of others, since we understand how they are tools for regulating our bodies' physical states of being and shaping our identity.

"Change what you say and it will change what you see."
-Dr. Myron Golden

THE POWER OF USING MUSIC AND RHYTHM WITH OUR WORDS

Do you remember how you learned your ABC's? You sang them. Was this true for your multiplication tables as well? Many of us learned how to skip count, multiply, and list the state capitals through music. Why does music have this unparalleled ability to help us remember data, profoundly experience an event, and take us to higher heights in our emotions?

Well, the world of neuroscience is currently answering that question.

Music activates multiple areas of the brain at the same time. It also activates areas in both hemispheres, or sides, of the brain. When you are engaged in music, you are giving your brain a full neural workout! When you are singing, chanting, or playing a musical instrument, the auditory, emotional, motor, and reward centers of the brain join in on the action. This is probably why information put to music is remembered better and with greater accuracy. I believe declarative statements put to music, and repeated over and over again, get stored in our nonconscious mind more effectively. This is a component of a concept called Neural Linguistic Programming, (NLP).

This concept suggests that words, lyrics, or statements placed over music and repeated many times seep into our sub and nonconscious mind as truth. These truths shape our belief system and how we see the world. This will eventually affect our behavior.

This is why we need to be aware of which musical lyrics we are singing to and listening to. If you are singing negative, derogatory words about yourself or others, that 'truth' seeps into your subconscious brain. This can affect your identity, your biases, and your perceptions of others.

This affects YOU!

When creating our declarations, we take these positive words and put a musical and rhythmic melody to them. Yes! We're rockin' and rollin' with our declarations, and our subconscious mind is recording it all.

THE POWER OF USING MOVEMENT WITH OUR WORDS

Don't just sit there and say the words. Get up and move too! We like to clap our hands and move our bodies when we declare these powerful words over our lives. Our framework of NeuroSomatic Creativity® discusses how our body is an instrument of thought. When we involve our whole body to engage in concert with our brain and our mind, the impact of our words travels much deeper into our essence. Our internal self sings and moves along with us.

This movement activates our cerebellum, which is involved with movement and balance. We also know the cerebellum helps monitor our prefrontal cortex, which is responsible for our executive functions. This includes our decision making, imagination, and emotional regulation. There are so many advantages to moving with the message. The beat helps these truths make their way into our belief system. I AM DILIGENT! I AM CREATIVE! Moving together also helps my family bond together as well.

Why? Entrainment.

Interpersonal entrainment, or moving together in time, has been shown to cultivate pro-social behaviors with the ones who are moving together. Basically, when we move together, we groove together which causes us to work better together. We are more likely to shift to the other person's perspective, honor their agency, and be more empathetic. Yes, the rhythm is gonna getcha … to cooperate!

Rhythm is very important for brain development in every life stage, from infancy to the elderly. Rhythmic perception develops early in life, and babies are sensitive to changes in patterns and changes to the beat. Rhythmic exercises are also used to help the elderly who are suffering with neurodegenerative diseases that affect movement, such as Parkinson's disease.

Once again, rhythm also allows for entrainment, which is moving to the beat with others. When we move to the beat, this allows us to entrain with the people we are doing our declarations with. When we move in time with another person, it causes us to like, trust, and cooperate with that person more. Teams, students, and families that move together, groove together, and GROW together!

THE POWER OF SYMBOLIC REPRESENTATION OF A CONCEPT

Symbols and metaphors are all around us, and they can be a part of your positive affirmation practice too. There is a raft of research on how the brain uses symbolic representation to increase understanding and store information. They also activate your imagination. Just look at the root of the word, 'Imagination'.

IMAGE

Since moving is effective for entrainment, another idea you can employ in your daily, weekly, or monthly declarations is to choreograph different symbolic movements for each declaration.

What does it look like to be BOLD? How do you adjust your body to communicate the idea of GRATEFULNESS? What pose does CURIOSITY bring about and why? In our NeuroSomatic Creativity® trainings, we call this 'rendering it into physical form'. We are rendering a conceptual abstract concept into a physical tangible representation. That is a creative skill. These are great movement prompts and discussion points to really dive into these words you are declaring into your life.

> *"Language is not just descriptive, it's creative. It raises people up, and it enables people to find out who they really are."*
> -Chief Rabbi Dr. Jonathon Sacks

POSITIVE DECLARATIONS (AFFIRMATIONS) ARE BENEFICIAL FOR OUR BRAINS

Remember the 1980's commercial where they opened a raw egg and said, "This is your brain." Then they cracked open another raw egg, slopped it into a hot frying pan, and warned, "And this is your brain on drugs." Sizzle Sizzle.

Well, let me give you a more optimistic image of your brain on something. Not on drugs, but on declaring positive affirmations over your life. There is fMRI evidence suggesting that certain neural pathways are increased when people practice self-affirmation tasks. If you want to be super specific, the ventromedial prefrontal cortex—involved in positive valuation and self-related information processing—becomes more active when we consider our personal values.

Research suggests that when we choose to practice positive affirmations, we're better able to view otherwise threatening information as more self-relevant and valuable. This can have several benefits because it relates to how we process information about ourselves and our ability to be resilient.

Declarations also help with reframing situations and seeing the silver lining in certain events. As inherently positive statements, affirmations are designed to encourage a hopeful mindset. Hope in itself is a powerful thing. In terms of reducing negative thoughts, affirmations have been shown to help lower the tendency to linger on negative experiences.

When we can deal with negative messages and replace them with positive statements, we can construct more adaptive, hopeful narratives about who we are and what we can accomplish. When we recite them with others, neurochemicals like oxytocin come into play. This can influence our perception of their potential as well. When we see the good in people, we see the hope in people.

DECLARATIONS AS A STARTING POINT

Some people might not agree fully with the idea of affirmations or positive declarations. They might think that people believe things just appear or behavior just changes automatically once you speak it out. I can understand that. To me, our declarations are a starting point. You act in accordance with what you believe. Our declarations are a part of our family reprogramming our subconscious mind to focus on the truths we want to see become a reality in our lives.

Nevertheless, we don't just say them and forget about them right afterward. We remember the words. We interact with the words. We bring the words to life.

Here are some ideas to bring your declarations to life.

We choose a word every week and intentionally focus on making it a quantifiable reality in our lives. This means we take it from the abstract and break it down into actionable items. For example, the declarations, 'I am KIND, or 'I am COMPASSIONATE,' are declarations that involve action. How have we been kind this past week? Can we increase our social network of who we are kind to? Does our compassion have a target? What is the true motivation for our compassion? How can our compassion be more creative? What is one thing we can do this next week to exhibit kindness and compassion?

To make these declarations take flight in your life, choose one to interact with throughout the week. Set intentional actions, due dates, and creative methods to make these declarations come alive.

CONTINUING YOUR OWN 'I AM' JOURNEY

Life is a journey, and so is this process. These sixteen declarative words are the words our family selected when we began our journey of speaking declarations as a family. You can start with these words, but we encourage you to change some, delete some, and add others depending on the words that resonate with you, your group, or your family. They may evolve as the season you are in continues to evolve.

Thank you for allowing us to share our declarative and affirmation journey with you. Creatively combining and using your words will help you build a road toward an adventurous destiny. The bold journey of discovery and learning never ends. Remember your words matter because they ARE matter. Let your words build the road that can lead you, your team and your family to endless possibilities.

I AM proud of you!

Creatively,

Shawn, Shayne, and Genein Marie Letford

'Create and Grow' Podcast
By Genein Letford

Episodes on Neuroscience and Creativity

- *How Neuroscience Is Informing Leadership, DE&I and Intercultural Creativity for this New Era*
  –Dr. Michael Platt, Episode #66

- *The Neuroscience of Education: How to Empower Our Students by Teaching with the Brain in Mind*
  -Dr. Kieran O'Mahoney, Episode #96

- *The Business of Your Brain: How Neuroscience Gives Us Insight In Decisions and Imagination*
  –Dr. Moran Serf, Episode #79

- *The Neuroscience of Mindfulness, Meditation, and the Power of the Creative Brain*
  –Dr. Nicole Tetreault, Episode #99

- *The Neuroscience of Our Health, Our Arts and Our Freedom Ride*
  -Dr. Peter Sterling, Episode #90

Listen to the full episodes on www.CAFFEstrategies.com/podcast

References

Barrett, L.F., (2020) Seven and a Half Lessons About the Brain, Houghton Mifflin Harcourt

Cascio, C. N., O'Donnell, M. B., Tinney, F. J., Lieberman, M. D., Taylor, S. E., Strecher, V. J., & Falk, E. B. (2016). Self-affirmation activates brain systems associated with self-related processing and reward and is reinforced by future orientation. *Social Cognitive and Affective Neuroscience*, 11(4), 621-629.

Cooke, R., Trebaczyk, H., Harris, P., & Wright, A.J. (2014) Self-affirmation promotes physical activity. *Journal of Sport and Exercise Psychology*, 36(2), 217–223.

Critcher, C. R., & Dunning, D. (2015). Self-affirmations provide a broader perspective on self-threat. *Personality and Social Psychology Bulletin*, 41(1), 3-18.

Epton, T., & Harris, P. R. (2008). Self-affirmation promotes health behavior change. *Health Psychology*, 27(6), 746-752.

Kraus, N. (2021) Of Sound Mind: How Our Brain Constructs a Meaningful Sonic World. MIT Press

Leaf, C. (2023). *How to Help Your Child Clean Up their Mental Mess: A Guide to Building Resilience and Managing Health*. Baker Books

Praise For *The Power of I AM*

"To <u>BE</u> starts with <u>I AM</u>! I have been using affirmations with my children since they were in kindergarten. We started with a simple list and my boys added their own. We called them the 'I AM and I CHOOSE' statements! Thank you for encouraging people of all ages to use their words with wisdom. My sons are now in high school and we still say them regularly!"

Goeff McLachlan,
Professionals at Play, Keynote Speaker

" 'The Power of I AM' Inner Child's book is both magical and compelling. Magical in its artistic beauty as each illustration conveys layers of insight and subtle images that support deeper conversations about being BLESSED, LOVED, WORTHY, CONFIDENT, HEALTHY, along with the other affirmations. Compelling in its articulation of current neuroscience research supporting the power of our words. The authors cover detailed material in understandable ways, creating a fundamental understanding that naturally flows from one scientist's perspective to the next. Readers of all ages will be inspired and motivated to declare their own I AM affirmations, knowing they are positively supporting themselves and those around them!"

Amy Camie, CTM-CCM,
Certified Therapeutic-Clinical Musician,
TEDxStLouis & Keynote Speaker

"If you think children (and adults) should hold value to words like Blessed, Kind, Respectful, Bold, and Creative, then 'The Power of I Am' will be great for your young child (and for you too)!"

Erik Seversen,
Best Selling Author, Keynote Speaker

"This brilliant book is aesthetically pleasing for all walks of life, through imagery, art, and healing affirmations. The book surpasses the adage 'a picture is worth 1000 words' with the turn of every page. As a licensed Marriage and Family Therapist, imagery and affirmation are necessary to assist clients in communicating deep rooted feelings, and emotions that could not be articulated at a moment's notice. This book will fill your emotional cup spilling and brimming with captivating affirmations for the soul. I highly recommend this brilliant book, The Power of I Am."

Nichole Henderson,
Life Strategist and Licensed Therapist

Partial proceeds of this book will benefit our diamond friends with arts education at the New Friends Homeless Center as well as teachers on Donorschoose.org. Visit www.newfriendshomelesscenter.org and Donorschoose.org to support these organizations today!

Genein M. Letford, M.Ed

As the 2019 LA Lakers Business Woman and the 2015 CA Charter Teacher of the Year, Genein is a national thought leader and creator of the concept of 'Intercultural Creativity®, NeuroSomatic Creativity®' and Prismatic Leadership®. She is the Founder and Chief Creative Officer of CAFFE Strategies, Inc which is a consulting, coaching, and training company that trains C-Suite executives and employees to create sustainable organizational creative and inclusive strategies, based on neuroscience, while unleashing their innovative thinking for themselves and in their businesses.

Her 7 Gems of Intercultural Creativity® is a leading framework that encourages corporations in their inclusion development while developing critical cognitive tools for creative thinking. Her first book, From Debt To Destiny: Creating Financial Freedom From the Inside Out connects creative thinking to financial agility and was an international bestseller in 5 finance categories. Her book, 7 Gems of Intercultural Creativity: Connecting, Creating and Innovating Across Cultural Lines is the only book on this topic. She published her 'Inner Child' (children's books), I AM CREATIVE and My Brain My Brain My Beautiful Brain with her 6-year-old son, Shawn Letford, and her husband, Shayne. Her next leadership book, Your Brain, Your Bias, and the Beauty of Your Creative Mind is due out next year. Genein believes creative thinking thrives best in an inclusive environment and she is often called 'America's Creative Coach' for her work in reigniting intercultural creativity within our students and our adult workforce.

Shayne Letford

With a degree in computer engineering, Shayne Letford began his design career in 2009. To date, Letford Media has designed websites, branding materials, video media and book covers for several companies throughout the world. My Brain My Brain was his first illustration project and, with the character support of Briefstock, Shayne composed 18 beautiful illustrations for the book. Shayne is the Director of Technology and Branding for CAFFE Strategies, INC. He lives in Arizona with his creative and adventurous family.

Shawn 'The Creative Kid' Letford

Shawn is a boy of many words. Publishing his first book, I AM CREATIVE, at three years old, Shawn is on a mission to help the world 'Be More Creative'. He goes through his daily life giving his parents pure examples of creative thinking, funny vocabulary, and inventive associations. He still enjoys sprinklers but has sparked an interest in flying drones, Sonic the HedgeHog, and engineering. He loves being observant and plays his piano and recorder to exercise his mind. He's taken the stage to share about creative thinking and would love to visit your school or organization! A non-fiction book about sprinklers or drones will be his first solo literary project.

Victoria Mappala

Victoria Mappala is a mixed media artist fueled by the awe and wonder of what colors can create. Victoria has been painting since she was old enough to pick up a brush. Recently, Victoria has expanded her craft into digital art and illustration. This new medium gives her the freedom and platform to explore and experiment with art in a new way, no longer limited by what can be created within a canvas.

Art has been an extension of the inner peace she experiences while creating. Her passion is to share and express that peace and life-giving hope through her artwork. Her mission is to show beauty in what may be seen as battered, treasure in the ordinary, and light in the darkness. This is her first children's book. She resides in Southern California with her husband, two children, and two dogs.

Other Books
By The Authors

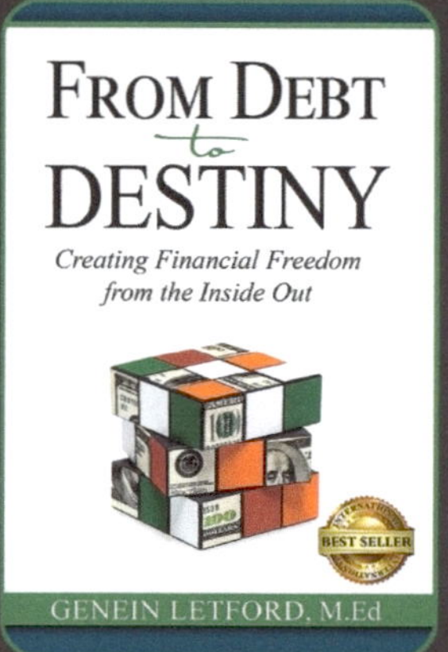

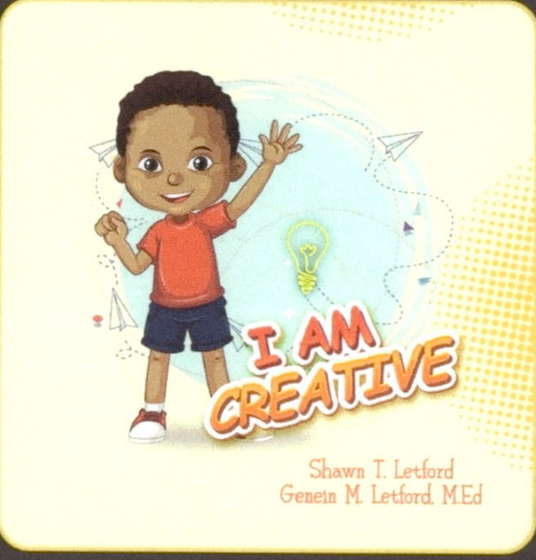

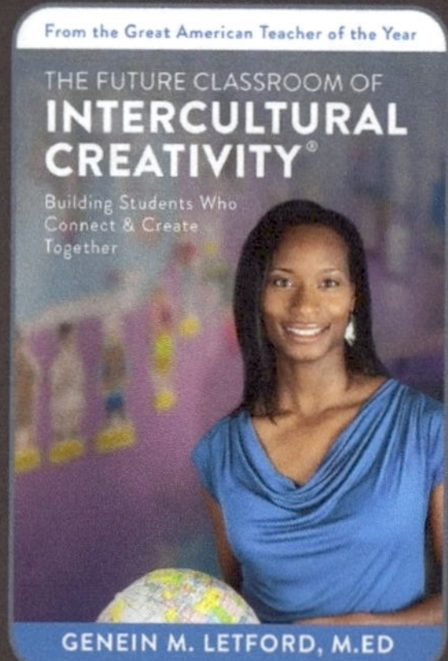

For more information, visit www.CAFFEstrategies.com

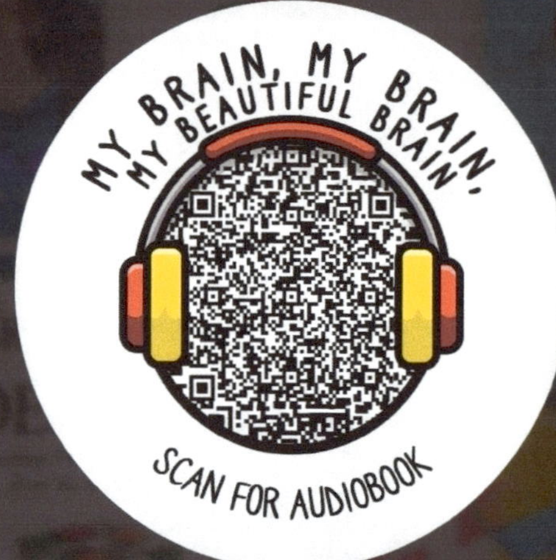

Professional Development for Companies, Organizations, and School Districts

Prismatic Leadership® Series

POWER, POSITION AND PURPOSE: UNDERSTANDING POWER DYNAMICS WHILE BUILDING INCLUSIVE TEAMS

Prismatic Leadership® is complex. Brain research shows that authoritative power can inhibit leaders from seeing the plight of others. This power can lower their ability for connection, creativity and cultural awareness. Since creativity needs psychological safety, intellectual humility, curiosity and empathy to flourish, effective leaders must be aware of how power, position and authority can skew their perspective. Learn brain-based strategies to mitigate the effects of power and become an efficient Prismatic Leader®.

THE NEUROSCIENCE OF LEADERSHIP: BUILDING A CULTURE OF TRUST IN DIVERSE TEAMS

The science is clear: Trust is the new driver of productivity. Communicating your message, lowering fears (both rational and irrational), and pulling out the best of your team members requires strong Prismatic Leadership® skills. Scientists have identified the brain mechanisms that support our ability to connect and communicate with others, revealing how we can activate and strengthen them. Learn how to develop team chemistry and trust by building team identity through shared goals, values and social connection.

EMPATHETIC LEADERSHIP: BUILDING CULTURAL SENSITIVITY AND CURIOSITY

Emotions lead, productivity follows; at least in the brain. Having a strong emotional foundation and understanding of the neuroscience behind how emotions work is an important aspect of emotional intelligence. Leaders will increase their emotional granularity (how to identify their emotions)

and regulation. They will learn how to use these identifications for Intercultural Creativity® and leadership. This training uses interactive and reflective exercises for deep transformational learning in areas such as perspective shifting, curiosity development, vulnerability and empathy.

REFLECTIVE LEADERSHIP: IMPROVE SELF-AWARENESS, RESILIENCE & AUTHENTICITY

Being able to understand yourself in uncertain times is an integral part of understanding and leading others. Improving brain based reflective practices that develop self-awareness, agile resilience and authenticity is now your most critical skill in this uncertain landscape. Prismatic Leaders will learn and implement the 5 elements of a resilient mindset and practice how to exercise these skills in various work experiences.

INTERCULTURAL CREATIVITY® FOR EDUCATORS

In times like these, educators need to be culturally sensitive and creative with their lessons and their engagement strategies with students. Teaching diverse students calls for engaging brain centric designed curriculum. Recognizing that culturally responsive instruction helps educators close achievement gaps, CAFFE Strategies offers programs that expands the capacity of educators to serve students from diverse cultural and ethnic backgrounds while increasing creativity at the same time.

NEUROSOMATIC CREATIVITY® IN THE CLASSROOM

To think creativity is only about the arts is wrong but to think one can reach their full creative potential without the arts is also incorrect. The creative arts (visual arts, dance, theatre and music) are integral parts of the human learning experience. Our unique NeuroSomatic Creativity® training guides educators through effective methods for integrating the creative arts within an established curriculum for increased engagement and exploration of the content.

This training specializes in connecting the neuroscience of the arts to metaphorical thinking, sensory observation, abstraction and more! Genein Letford has successfully lectured on arts integration at the university level and is pleased to bring her specialized program to educators across the nation. Let's get our students moving, painting, playing, creating and learning through the arts!

Certification programs are available. Visit CAFFEstrategies.com for more information.